BREEZE OF THE GODS:

THE MYTHOLOGY, HISTORY, AND COMPLICATIONS OF PERFUME IN
ANCIENT GREECE

DON ARP, JR.

Published in Australia
BIC Classification:
ACG (History of Art: Ancient and Classical), HRKP3 (Ancient Greek
Mythology), 1QDAG (Ancient Greece), HDDK (Greek Archeology), WJH
(Beauty).
978-0-9875598-8-3

NUMEN BOOKS
WWW.NUMENBOOKS.COM

BREEZE OF THE GODS

The Mythology, History, and Complications
of Perfume in Ancient Greece

DON ARP, JR., MA

CONTENTS

ABOUT THE AUTHOR

DON ARP, JR., has an M.A. in Anthropology and a B.A. with Highest Distinction in History, both from the University of Nebraska-Lincoln, and a Certificate in Forensic Science from North Central State College in Mansfield, Ohio. Don is published in several fields and has had his work cited in three textbooks and a *New York Times* bestseller. In 2007, his work as a volunteer civilian consultant and historian of U.S. military operations, especially those in post-Hurricane Katrina Louisiana, was recognized with the U.S. Army Commander's Award for Public Service.

8

ACKNOWLEDGMENTS

THE NUCLEUS OF this work was a term paper for an archaeology class I took in the Spring of 2000. It subsequently became the focus of the research I conducted in partial completion of the requirements of attaining Highest Distinction at the University of Nebraska-Lincoln in 2001. Several people deserve special thanks for their assistance, ideas, and encouragement during the writing of this work. My undergraduate honors thesis advisors, Dr. Michael Hoff (Department of Art and Art History, University of Nebraska-Lincoln) and Dr. Jessica Coope (Department of History, University of Nebraska-Lincoln), without whom I would have never been able to complete this project. Dr. Thomas Rinkevich (Department of Classics and Religious Studies, University of Nebraska-Lincoln) and Zach Schroeder deserve significant thanks for their help, interest, and encouragement.

Any errors found in this text are my responsibility and should not reflect upon them in any way.

Don Arp, Jr., MA
Lincoln, NE
November 2014

DEDICATION

THIS WORK IS dedicated to Ur-e11-e, the Sumerian scribe who wrote the clay tablet that introduced me to the world of ancient perfume and led me to ask the question whose answer was larger than I could have ever anticipated.

I. INTRODUCTION

Archaeology and history have, over the past two centuries, been concerned not so much with the life of the average person in the ancient world, nor the detailed social phenomena that impacted their life. A renaissance occurred during the last decades of the twentieth century that allowed social history and archaeology to enter upon an age of serious investigation. Social phenomena that were once thought of as trivial are now coming to the forefront of the field and shedding light on cultures academia once thought it thoroughly knew. One of these social phenomena, perfume, was one of the most written about subjects in the ancient world. Modern interest and scholarship has been sporadic, often leaving many questions and topics unanswered. Perfume was a vital facet of ancient life, especially in ancient Greece. Perfume permeated Greek society and culture, integrating itself into almost every part of daily life. Bathing, medicine, and religious worship all incorporated perfume and other fragrant substances.

This broad spectrum of involvement created a system of trade and social relationships that not only tied Greece to the outside world, but aided a system of social divisions that stratified the society of ancient Greek civilization.

Fragrant materials abounded in the ancient world. Incense, perfume, unguents, and other scented substances were numerous in variety and price. The word 'perfume' comes from the Latin *per* meaning 'through' and *fumus*, meaning 'smoke'.[1] This name gives a clue as to the original use of aromatic substances. As will be discussed later, fire, used with incense and in the production of perfume, is the key ingredient to the manufacture of aromatic substances. The Greeks usually used the term *myra* to refer to perfume. Other names existed, but the Greeks preferred to refer to the substance by its specific name. Names for Greek perfumes had three sources: the geographic location of its main ingredient or invention (ex. Rhodinum); the main ingredient (ex. Crocinum); or the name of the manufacturer (ex. Megaleion after Megallus).[2] The Greeks also used another fragrant substance, a more paste-like concoction known as an unguent. These salves were medicinal rather than cosmetic, but no

[1] JOHN TRUEMAN, *The Romantic Story of Scent* (Garden City, NJ: Doubleday and Company, 1975), 65.

[2] FRANCIS KENNETT, *History of Perfume* (London: George G. Harrap and Co., 1975), 67.

less important to the Greeks. Indeed, there is overlap between unguents and perfumes in the medicinal arts. The production of unguents did not have the social and economic implications that perfume production did. For this reason, perfume is the subject in need of investigation.

Perfume falls into a category that could be termed 'forgotten history'. Substances such as cosmetics, perfumes, some foods, and other hard to preserve cultural products tend to be forgotten. Their poor preservation makes archaeological investigations hard. Thankfully, ancient perfume has a rich archaeological record that had been interpreted, to a certain degree, in the past. Studies by Brun are reexamining perfume production through archaeology.[3] Regardless, perfume is an intriguing commodity in history. Often, when history and ancient peoples are pondered, smell is omitted along with the other senses. Granted, scholars like Sir Arthur Evans created elaborate reconstructions of ancient cities and cultures, but olfactory stimuli are oddly absent. Smell adds a certain dimension to an extinct culture. The substance and others like it have been around for several millennia. A Sumerian cuneiform tablet in the University of Nebraska State Museum Collection, dated to 2042 B.C., speaks

---

[3] JEAN-PIERRE BRUN, "The Production of Perfumes in Antiquity: The Cases of Delos and Paestum" in *American Journal of Archaeology*, 104 (2000), 277-308.

of perfume in ancient Umma.[4] Tablets in other collections, and of various dates, further elucidate the beginnings of perfume. Every major culture had aromatic substances, either in the form of incense, pastes, or perfumes. Egyptians, Assyrians, Hebrews, and other major civilizations had the knowledge and ability to produce these substances.[5] The concepts of perfume production may have diffused into Greece from other cultures, but it seems that the Greeks were primarily responsible for inventing the art in their own land. Foreign influence was not absent as many ingredients were of foreign origin.[6] Regardless, the Greeks made the art of perfumery their own and characteristically different from the methods practiced by other perfume manufacturing cultures.

The social and economic system that developed around perfume and its production created a unique time in which classic Greek ideals began to slide. These developments, criticized by many Greek intellectuals, forever changed the course of Greek civilization and may have accounted for its downfall. The myth, mystery, and factual evidence of ancient Greek perfume spins a telling tale worthy of investigation.

---

[4] DON ARP, JR., "Signs of the Times" in *Museum Notes*, February 2001 (108).

[5] EDWARD SAGARIN, *The Science and Art of Perfumery* (New York: McGraw-Hill Book Company, 1945), 1-15.

[6] KENNETT, 66.

For the most part, the period concerned is 5th century B.C. Greece. Any deviations from this time are obvious by context or given date.

II. MYTHOLOGICAL *&*
SECULAR ORIGIN

A s with most things in the ancient world, perfume was given a mythological origin. By studying the myths surrounding perfume, an understanding of the ancient Greek mind set can be gained. If one knows how the Greeks thought about perfume, then their actions make more sense. Context, as always, is the most important clue. Myth and beliefs are the glue that holds the complicated world of perfume together.

Varieties of references exist describing the nymph that taught humanity the art of perfumery, but clear primary source evidence is sketchy. Thus, establishing a reliable list of perfume myths and tracing their characters is complicated. Scholars during the last few centuries insisted on Latinizing (also Romanizing) Greek names and gods. This significantly complicates the issues, as the Latinizations are at times hard to follow.

The Greeks are said to have learned the art of perfumery from a river nymph named Aeone.[7] At first, due to a lack of sources and proper referencing, corroboration of this name proved difficult. It was unknown whether Thompson (1927) had made an error that Genders (1972) had unknowingly furthered. Genders' book lacked detailed referencing, so tracing his source was impossible. The same held true for Thompson. It seemed that the name Aeone might have been an invention using the Greek word *aiou - aw*, meaning to 'foment'.[8] This is closely tied with the concept of fomentation or applying hot, pain-relieving substances to the body. This could be construed as an unguent or perfumed paste. The problem could have been resolved if either author had properly referenced their source. However, the real problem lay not in their source, but in their Latinization of the nymph's name. It seems that the name Aeone came from the Greek name Oenone, who was taught the art of perfumery by Aphrodite.[9] Oenone was a river nymph born to

---

[7] ROY GENDERS, *Perfume Through the Ages* (New York: G. P. Putnam's Sons, 1972), 65; C. J. S. THOMPSON, *The Mystery and Lure of Perfume* (Philadelphia: J. B. Lippincott Company, 1927), 59.

[8] Consultation with Dr. Thomas Rinkevich, Department of Classics and Religious Studies, University of Nebraska-Lincoln.

[9] TRUEMAN, 81; EUGENE RIMMEL, *The Book of Perfumes* (London: Chapman and Hall, 1865), 82.

the river god Cebren.[10] Other sources say her father was Celsen.[11] How the Greeks received the knowledge of perfume manufacture from Oenone is a torrid tale of love and betrayal. Oenone, living on Mount Ida, fell in love with the mortal Paris (although she had no idea he was a mortal at that time).[12] Oenone received many gifts from the gods. Rhea (some sources say Apollo) gave her the ability to prophesy. Aphrodite, as mentioned before, gave her the secrets of perfume. Oenone passed these secrets on to Paris.[13] As time progressed, Paris betrayed Oenone by falling in love with, and then kidnapping, Helen. While at Troy, Paris gave Helen the secrets of perfume. Upon her return to Greece, Helen shared her knowledge with the Greek women.[14] Exactly why Oenone is tied to perfume is unclear. Trueman (1975) fails to reference his source. Possible evidence, however, can be found in Ovid's *Heroides*. In the letter from Oenone to Paris, it is written:

> Every helpful herb and every healing root,
> wherever it grows, is known to me.[15]

---

[10] APOLLODORUS (trans. by SIR JAMES FRAZER), *The Library* (Cambridge: Harvard University Press, 1921), 51.

[11] TRUEMAN, 83.

[12] GRANT, 304.

[13] TRUEMAN, 81.

[14] RIMMEL, 82.

[15] OVID (trans. by HAROLD ISBELL), *Heroides* (London: Penguin Books, 1990), 45.

The note given by the work's translator, Harold Isbell, states that Oenone learned this knowledge from Rhea. Knowledge of herbs and roots could easily be extrapolated into the realm of perfume, as many ingredients were herbs or roots. Further support to Oenone's medicinal abilities is recorded by Lycophron: "And herself [Oenone], the skilled with drugs..."[16] Inserting Aphrodite into the mix makes the transition from healing plants to perfumes complete. It may seem a scholastic stretch, but it is important to bear in mind that perfumes did have medicinal value in the ancient world. Indeed, this correlation between medicine and a superhuman being will be visited again.

The time line for Oenone's story is slightly off as the Greeks had knowledge of perfume before the Trojan War, but it serves as an adequate mythological foundation for the beginnings of perfume. Mythology is full of references to perfume and other aromatic substances. To fully recount every instance and story could easily fill several volumes. Thus, three characters will be focused on and their role in the mythology of perfume explained. The first character lacks a perfume myth. Philyra was the daughter of Oceanus and Tethys and mother of the centaur Chiron.[17] References to her as a goddess of perfume and paper abound on internet

---

[16] LYCOPHRON (trans. by G.R. MAIR) *Callimachus and Lycophron* (Cambridge: Harvard University Press, 1978), 325.

[17] APOLLODORUS, 13.

mythology pages, but textual verification is difficult to find. *The Oxford Classical Dictionary*, *Harper's Classical Dictionary*, and the *Pauly-Wissowa* are silent on the subject. Like Oenone, Philyra's link to perfume may be through the medicinal arts and the flowers of the tree she morphed into, the linden.[18] Her son, Chiron, was the wisest of the Centaurs and a skilled physician. Physicians in ancient Greece had a detailed knowledge of perfumes and unguents, making use of them to cure a variety of ills.

Most myths that pertain to perfume do not deal with it specifically, but rather with the origin of an ingredient. Two such stories are those of the Sun-God and Leucothoe, and Cinyras and Myrrha. The story of the Sun-God and Leucothoe is told in Ovid's *Metamorphoses*. The Sun-God was in love with a girl named Leucothoe. She was buried in a mountain and when she died and could not be resuscitated, the Sun turned her into frankincense.[19] Frankincense was an important aromatic substance in the ancient world. Primarily it was not used in perfume, but rather burned during religious rituals as incense and as a postmortem body treatment. The story does illustrate the importance of heat to the process of perfumery

---

[18] JOTHAM JOHNSON, *The New Century Classical Handbook* (New York: Appleton-Century-Crofts, Inc., 1962), 878.

[19] OVID (trans. by ROLFE HUMPHRIES), *Metamorphoses* (Bloomington: Indiana University Press, 1983), 87-90.

and incense. Without heat, the chemical concoctions used as perfume would not be as potent or usable.

The last myth to examine deals with an important perfume ingredient: myrrh. The story of Cinyras and Myrrha is one of forbidden lust. Aphrodite, for some unknown reproach, curses Myrrha to lust for her father.[20] Myrrha manages to enter her father's bedchamber and engage in sexual congress with him during several nights of marital abstinence required by a certain festival. Cinyras finds out what he has done and tries to kill her. Myrrha, pregnant, flees and is turned into a myrrh tree.[21] From the tree the youth Adonis is born. Myrrh is an important perfume ingredient and was much sought after in the Middle East and Mediterranean world. Its exotic odor and sources gave it a sense of mystery almost as alluring as frankincense. This story also introduces the holotype of a perfume user: the lover in the guise of Adonis.

Adonis was a young and very attractive boy. Aphrodite was in love with him and became his protector. It is important to know that, "Adonis is synonymous both with perfume and with the lover."[22] The two concepts are hard to separate. Adonis' carefree attitude and playboy mentality are

[20] GRANT, 116.

[21] OVID (trans. by ROLFE HUMPHRIES), 243-251.

[22] MARCEL DETIENNE (trans. by JANET LLOYD), *The Gardens of Adonis* (Atlantic Highlands, NJ: The Humanities Press, 1972), 63.

the personality characteristics that will be heavily criticized by perfume critics such as Socrates when they examine the damage done to Greek society by aromatic substances. Mythologically and secularly, perfume was an instrument of love. It could be used by the beautiful to make themselves irresistible. It could even make the most dispassionate become exceedingly amorous. Even Sappho, the poet of Lesbos, fell in love with a man because of his perfume.[23] Perfume, teamed with feminine wiles, could be used as a weapon. The story of Myrrhina or 'Little-Myrtle', is one such case. Aristophanes tells the story in the Lysistrata. The Greek women, wanting the war to end, deny their husbands sex. They make use of "...all the arms of their sex, 'your saffron dresses and your finical shoes, your paints and perfumes and your robes of gauze.'"[24] Myrrhina gets her husband to the bedchamber, but makes several excuses, first the bed is bad, then she protests no oil has been rubbed on. Myrrhina rubs herself down and gives the oil to her spouse. At this point, he is quite aroused, but Myrrhina escapes leaving him painfully frustrated. An important note must be made of the name Myrrhina. It does mean 'little-myrtle'. Crowns of this shrub were worn by marrying couples. Further, the name is used to refer to "either the clitoris or pudenda of the women. Thus the perfume in which Myrrhina

[23] GENDERS, 66; RIMMEL, 81

[24] DETIENNE, 62.

smothers herself is simply the ultimate expression of seductive attraction emanating from a woman totally committed to Aphrodite."[25] Another connection can be drawn here between Myrrhina (the pudendal definition) and fragrance. It has long been a practice of women in Brazil to avoid cleansing smegma from their reproductive orifice, as the odor produced is believed to be an alluring perfume of sorts. Whether any such practice is implied in this mythology is debatable, but possible. It must be remembered that in mythology and literature, the major function of perfume and unguents was for bathing and seduction, with bathing being carried out for reasons of lust and beguilement. In the secular world, perfume was more multi-faceted.

The mythological origins of perfume are clouded to be sure. This is, however, the nature of mythology. Stories change as they are passed on and travel through time and geography. Trying to find a synthesis of the myths that does not contradict itself is an impossible task. Thus, the myths and stories surrounding the origin of perfume must be taken as works of religion or literature, but can never be discounted as unimportant. Indeed, it was the secrecy fostered by a profit-minded secular world that breathed life into the sense of mystery and divine intervention found in the Greek myths and stories.

---

[25] DETIENNE, 63.

Near Eastern influence in perfume production in ancient Greece was noted by historians as being a product of Alexander the Great's military adventures and the subsequent "orientalization" of Greek culture.[26] The origins of perfumery knowledge in pre-Alexander Greece were lost until archaeologists began to discover the ancient civilizations on Crete and Cyprus. Discoveries of the Minoan civilization (2600 - 1250 B.C.) on Crete have shown that the civilization enjoyed the production and use of fragrant oils. The oils were shipped around the Mediterranean, usually to Egypt, by the seafaring Phoenicians. A usual companion of perfume on these trading voyages was opium.[27] Any other correlation between perfume and opium is nonexistent; however, some theories can be suggested. Opium was known to the Greeks as a pain reliever and possible recreational drug. Opium may have been, like perfume, a luxury product that was patronized by those who could afford it.

Crete was a natural location in which perfumery blossomed. The island had several plants that, at least in the ancient world, were aromatically pleasing. These plants included cumin, fennel, mint, sesame, *Pistacia terebinthos* (turpentine tree), and cyperus.[28] It

[26] EDWIN T. MORRIS, *Fragrance: The Story of Perfume from Cleopatra to Chanel* (New York: Charles Scribner's Sons, 1984), 75.

[27] MORRIS, 74.

[28] RODNEY CASTLEDEN, *Minoans: Life in Bronze Age Crete* (London: Routledge, 1990), 52.

also appears that coriander, a spice used in ancient and modern cooking, was also quite plentiful and popular in Minoan Knossos as a perfume ingredient. Texts from Knossos, Pylos, and Mycenae detail the dispersal of large quantities of coriander, with one tablet from Pylos making a specific reference to a so-called 'unguent-cooker'.[29] By trade routes, the Minoan perfumed oils and other materials were, as previously mentioned, sold around the Mediterranean and seem to have funded the opulent lifestyles of both Greek and Minoan cultures.[30] Exactly when Minoan knowledge of perfumery was transferred to the Mycenaeans is unclear, but Mycenaean success is quite obvious. Stirrup-jars, a design common to the Mycenaeans, are found all over the Mediterranean. These jars, postulated by some to be the forerunner to the lekythos, carried olive oil and aromatic oils alike.[31] Mycenaean success can be seen in the number of these vessels that are found and the luxury goods they purchased.

One would be grievously mistaken to assume that knowledge of perfumery was either completely

---

[29] JOHN CHADWICK, *The Mycenaean World* (London: Cambridge University Press, 1976), 119.

[30] LEONARD R. PALMER, *Mycenaeans and Minoans: Aegean Prehistory in the Light of the Linear B Tablets* (New York: Alfred A. Knopf, 1965), 21 & 113.

[31] PALMER, 113.

introduced to a civilization or was completely indigenous in invention. Although documentation of exactly when and how certain city-states and other political entities received perfumery knowledge is lacking, assumptions can be made that may explain the spread of the aromatic arts. It is true that perfume manufacturing occurred in Mesopotamia, the Levant, and Egypt, with the latter having the most influence on the Greek world. This knowledge was spread to surrounding areas where it either instigated or reformed the production of perfume. Exchange of knowledge was facilitated by a search for reliable sources of quality ingredients. As trade networks were established, reluctance on the part of the Phoenicians to reveal the sources of their spices and aromatics led to the discovery of domestic ingredients and the corresponding methods of manufacture. This process, although greatly localized in Greek city-states, was not completely isolated from outside influence, either domestic or foreign. The spread of perfume production can, at best, be described as a multi-faceted process involving development at several different levels and locations with the ultimate goals being to create substances that were exotic, mysterious, and pleasing.

As time progressed another factor, cost, would weigh into the fray and dramatically change the face of perfume and the Greek culture that used it, but this is a topic for another chapter.

III. PERFUME PRODUCTION

PERFUME PRODUCTION IN ancient Greece was controlled by the ingredients necessary for the fashionable concoction of the day. A great variety of flowers and spices were used as aromatic agents. These materials were placed in olive oil, balanos oil, or wine. Common practice in modern perfumery is to use alcohol as an excipient or evaporant.[32] It has a low evaporation point and thus can readily enter the air, along with molecules of the aromatic material. The ancient Greeks had no knowledge of alcohol's beneficial effects on perfume, thus placing it in wine was an accident and usually done for culinary purposes only.

The increased differentiation of ingredients charted progress for perfume technology and innovation. Sources like Rimmel (1865) say that the Greeks started their foray into perfume with flowered-scented oils and only made further progress with an influx of Near

---

[32] JEAN-PIERRE BRUN, "The Production of Perfumes in Antiquity: The Cases of Delos and Paestum" in *American Journal of Archaeology*, 104 (2000), 277-308.

Eastern knowledge.[33] If Near Eastern influence was great, the Greeks made a departure as they favored flower-based perfumes to the spice-based aromatics of the Near East.[34] The favoring of flowers did not eliminate the influence of spices. The Greeks used an impressive battery of spices and flowers to create much sought after fragrances, using materials and techniques that are still in use today. This 'aromatic arsenal' is known chiefly from the works of Apollonius of Herophila and Theophrastus. Together, their studies of perfume and aromatic materials serve as both cookbook and atlas for the perfumes and unguents of ancient Greece.

Although perfume varied in ingredients, general requirements did exist. The perfume had to consist of a stymmata or oil and the hedysmata or aromatics.[35] Other substances such as salt (a preservative), coloring agents, and thinning agents such as wines, water, and honey were used.[36] The use of wines and other liquids to thin the mixture was a mark of distinction for Greek perfumers, as their Near Eastern and Egyptian predecessors preferred animal fats.[37]

---

[33] RIMMEL, 82.

[34] KENNETT, 70.

[35] KENNETT, 69.

[36] KENNETT, 70.

[37] KENNETT, 70.

The key ingredient to any perfume are the spices and flowers used to make the substance's pleasing bouquet. A variety of spices and flowers were used: cassia, cinnamon, cardamom, spikenard, balsam of Mecca, storax, iris, costus, saffron, crocus, oenanthe, ginger-grass, marjoram, lotus, dill, quince, origanum, thyme, and fennel.[38] The breath of substances used in perfume was best described by Theophrastus when he wrote:

Perfumes are compounded from various parts of the plant, flowers leaves twigs root wood fruit and gum: and in most cases the perfume is made from a mixture of several parts. Rose and gilliflower perfumes are made from the flowers: so also is the perfume called susinon, this too being made from flowers, namely, lilies: also the perfumes named from bergamot-mint and tufted thyme, kypros, and also the saffron-perfume; the crocus which produces this is best in Aegina and Cilicia. Instances of those made from the leaves are the perfumes called from myrtle and drop-wort: this grows in Cyprus on the hills and is very fragrant: that which grows in Hellas yields no perfume, being scentless.

---

[38] KENNETT, 70.

From roots are made the perfumes named from iris spikenard and sweet marjoram, an ingredient in which is koston; for it is the root to which this name is applied. The Eretrian unguent is made from the root of kypeiron, which is obtained from the Cyclades as well as from Euboea. From wood is made what is called 'palm-perfume' : for they put in what is called the 'spathe,' having first dried it. From fruits are made the quince-perfume, the myrtle, and the bay. The 'Egyptian' is made from several ingredients, including cinnamon and myrrh.[39]

Spices were, in practice, more sought after than flowers and other substances for perfumes.

They use spices in the making of all perfumes; some to thicken the oil, some in order to impart their odor. For in all cases they thicken the oil to some extent to make it take the odor better, just as they treat wool for dyeing. The less powerful spices are used for the thickening, and then at a later stage they put in the one whose odor they wish to secure. For that which is put in last always dominates, even if it is in small quantity; thus, if a pound of myrrh is put into a half-pint of oil, and at a later stage a

[39] THEOPHRASTUS (trans. by SIR ARTHUR HORT), *Enquiry Into Plants and Minor Works on Odours and Weather Signs* (London: William Heinemann, 1916), 351 & 353.

third of an ounce of cinnamon is added, this small amount dominates.[40]

These materials, spice and flower alike, would either be pressed in a torsion-type device or soaked to release their aromatic oils or essences.

The biggest problem facing perfumers was consistency, especially in regard to spices. There was, as has been observed, a wide variety of spices and flowers used in the manufacture of perfume. The sources of these substances stayed fairly stable, but quality control was always an issue. Potency of a particular spice could depend on any number of factors such as temperature, sunlight, precipitation, and soil chemistry. Theophrastus addresses the problem of quality and lays down three factors that must be considering when trying to preserve ingredient strength and character: season, time of collection, and aging.[41] It was hoped that by using these parameters, ingredient integrity would be preserved. However, these guidelines did not remove the inconsistency of the perfume manufacturing process. Subtle differences in chemistry could make one batch of perfume smell dramatically different from another. Constant revision of recipes and methods probably made these mistakes an increasing rarity.

---

[40] THEOPHRASTUS, 343.

[41] THEOPHRASTUS, 361.

Perfumes did not always contain only one spice or flower as the source of their fragrance. Ancient perfumers practiced the art of compounding, a process still used in modern perfumery. Compounding refers to making a scent out of several constituent materials. These different spices are hydrated with wine and placed in some kind of closed box or other vessel. After a specified length of time, a spice is removed if it becomes to over-powering. A "general scent derived from all" ingredients is the goal of compounding perfume.[42] The scent created with this process makes the most sought after perfumes. It also seems that the concept of compounding was used with perfumes themselves. People often wore more than one perfume at a time in order to create a certain aromatic montage.

Another important ingredient in perfume, perhaps even more important than the spices and flowers, is the oil base. As was previously mentioned, the fact that alcohol could be used as an excipient or evaporant was unknown to the Greeks. Oil, capable of capturing odors from a variety of substances, was used. The fat molecules in the oil attached themselves to the aromatic oils and essences found in flowers and spices. Not only could oil hold a compounded fragrance, but also it lasted longer than other substances and was easy to apply.[43] Two oils were used in the production

---

[42] THEOPHRASTUS, 377 & 379.

[43] THEOPHRASTUS, 343.

of perfume: olive and balanos. Olive oil was not the most desired for perfumery, but some varieties of it were useful. As Brun (2000) described, it could be processed on a large scale or simply crushed in a mortar and processed in small amounts.[44] Oil pressed from raw, coarse olives was deemed as the best olive oil as it had less detritus and was not as greasy as other varieties.[45] Although olive oil was convenient and thus available in large quantities, the Egyptian oil called balanos was more revered for its perfume making quality. Theophrastus himself denotes balanos oil (*Balanites aegyptica*) as the most used perfume oil:

The oil most used is that derived from the Egyptian or Syrian balanos, since this is the least viscous.[46]

Thus the oil which is most receptive, for instance, that of the Egyptian balanos, will also keep the longest, and for the same reason; namely that that oil which is most receptive unites, more than others, into one single substance, as it were, with the spices. Such a substance will always last longer than others.[47]

---

[44] BRUN, 287.

[45] THEOPHRASTUS, 341.

[46] THEOPHRASTUS, 341.

[47] THEOPHRASTUS, 345.

Even though balanos oil was sought after, some aromatic substances did not react well with it. Indeed, rose-perfume had to be made with sesame-oil as it was more 'viscid'.[48]

Once all the ingredients were assembled, processing was necessary. Some spices and other aromatics required boiling or soaking. Heating is required to make spices astringent.[49] The method of heating the perfume mixture is important to note. The perfume was placed in a vessel and in turn placed in a water filled vessel. This second vessel actually contacted the fire. The water surrounding the perfume container was brought to a boil. This process saved the perfume from direct and harmful contact with the fire. Any over-heating that could be caused by fire contact would make the perfume smell burned and was thus undesirable.[50]

Once the proper amount of spice or other aromatics were mixed and stewed in the heated oil, a few final preparations were necessary. The oil, especially balanos, would do a good job of picking up the aromatic molecules of the constituent spices, but preservability was questionable. Preservatives such as storax, boiled from a tree, were used to 'fix' a perfume's

---

[48] THEOPHRASTUS, 345.

[49] THEOPHRASTUS, 347

[50] THEOPHRASTUS, 347.

odor.[51] Some authors hint at other preservatives, but refuse to name them. When thinking of perfume, we think of the yellowish liquids we encounter in department stores and the like. It is easy to forget that color is an important facet to a substance like perfume, especially in the ancient world. Theophrastus writes:

> Some perfumes are made up colorless, some are given colour. They give colour to sweet majoram-perfume, rose-perfume, and megaleion, while among expensive kinds the Egyptian, quince-perfume and kypros are colourless, as well as all the cheaper kinds. The reason why these are made without colour is that it is desired that the Egyptian and kypros should look white and that quince-perfume should have the colour of quinces, while it is not worth while to add colour to the cheaper sorts. They dye used for colouring red perfumes is alkanet; the sweet majoram-perfume is dyed with the substance called khroma (dye), which is a root imported from Syria.[52]

The finished product would be stored out of sunlight and away from direct heat, usually in larger vessels from which it would be decanted into smaller personalized pieces. Formulas and procedures varied.

---

[51] GENDERS, 76-77.

[52] THEOPHRASTUS, 355.

"The ancient texts of these formulas and recipes are imprecise, particularly in terms of instruments, processes, and quantities."[53] Thankfully, the process used to create one of the more popular perfumes, megaleion, is known and well recorded. It serves as a case study in understanding the complete perfume manufacturing process.

Megaleion was made and named by the perfumer Megallus.[54] Megaleion was one of the most expensive perfumes available on the ancient Greek market. It consisted of the most expensive materials: balanos, burnt resin, myrrh oil, cinnamon, and cassia. The first step in the manufacturing process of megaleion was to boil the balanos for ten days in order to remove any impurities.[55] Burnt resin was then added to the boiled balanos. Myrrh was the next ingredient to be processed. Depending on the account, it would seem that megaleion actually contained another perfume known as myrrh-oil. The oily part of myrrh, called *stakte*, was used in megaleion.[56] According to Theophrastus, this was a perfume in and of itself. He writes of stakte production:

---

[53] BRUN, 277.

[54] KENNETT, 67.

[55] THEOPHRASTUS, 353 & 355.

[56] THEOPHRASTUS, 353.

...but others declare that the manufacture of stakte (myrrh-oil) is as follows: having bruised the myrrh and dissolved it in oil of balanos over a gentle fire, they pour hot water on it: and the myrrh and oil sink to the bottom like a deposit; and, as soon as this has occurred, they strain off the water and squeeze the sediment in a press.[57]

Once the myrrh-oil was produced, the cinnamon and cassia were mixed with it. Finally, this concoction of myrrh-oil and spices was added to the balanos and resin mixture. A final touch of color was added with alkanet (*Anchusa tinctoria*).[58] The final product was expensive, but apparently well worth the price.

Not all perfumes were produced in the same location. Factors such as trade networks and availability of ingredients played a role in regional perfume specialization. Archaeology, through the discovery of perfume shops and myriads of pottery vessels, has shown how widespread the industry was, but it does not necessarily shed light on what perfumes were produced where. Thankfully, Apollonius, an ancient scholar of perfume, gives a clue and elucidates the most important control on perfume quality: the perfumer. Apollonius writes:

---

[57] THEOPHRASTUS, 353.

[58] KENNETT, 69.

The iris is best in Elis and at Cyzicus; the perfume made from roses is most excellent at Phaselis, and that made at Naples and Capua is also very fine. That made from crocus (saffron) is in the highest perfection at Soli in Cilicia, and at Rhodes. The essence of spikenard is best at Tarsus, and the extract of vine-leaves is made best at Cyprus and at Adramyttium. The best perfume from marjoram and from apples comes from Cos. Egypt bears the palm for its essence of Cyprius, and the next best is the Cyprian and Phoenician, and after them comes the Sidonaian. The perfume called Panathenaicum is made at Athens, and those called Metopian and Mendesian are prepared with the greatest skill in Egypt. But the Metopian is made from oil which is extracted from bitter almonds. Still, the superior excellence of each perfume is owing to the purveyors, and materials, and the artist, and not to the place itself, for Ephesus formerly, as men say, had a high reputation for the excellence of its perfumery, and especially of its megallium, but now it has none. At one time, too, the unguents made in Alexandria were brought to high perfection on account of the wealth of the city and the attention that Arisnoe and Berenice paid to such matters; and the finest extract of roses in the world was made at Cyrene while the great Berenice was alive. Again, in ancient times the extract of vine-leaves made at Adramyttium was but poor; but afterwards it became first-rate, owing to Stratonice, the wife of Eumenes. Formerly, too, Syria used to make every sort of unguents admirably, especially that extracted from fenugreek, but the case is quite altered now. And long ago there used to be a most delicious unguent extracted from frankincense at Pergamus, owing to the invention of a certain perfumer of that city, for no one else had made it before him; but now none is made there.[59]

As was previously mentioned, Apollonius is the chief source for the study of regional perfume variation. Other ancient authors either disregarded the entire subject or dealt with it on an ingredients basis alone. Saying that one geographical location has the best roses does not mean that it made the best rose-perfume. As Apollonius correctly points out, success laid in the hands of a talented perfumer. It could be added that the talented perfumer needed quality ingredients.

The Greeks developed perfumery as their own art, with influence in methods and ingredients from their ancient Near Eastern and Egyptian predecessors. By refining their art, the Greeks incorporated more indigenous ingredients and developed new methods to produce highly sought after substances. Most of the 'recipes' for the perfumes have been lost, with

---

[59] RIMMEL, 83 & 84.

a few notable exceptions. Regardless, a detailed list of ingredients is known to scholarship and serves as the sole basis for understanding ancient olfactory preferences. Some regions, usually due to talented perfumers, specialized in certain perfumes. These specializations were not solid, but changed as perfumers died off and trade routes expired. One thing that did not die off, however, was the demand for perfumes and unguents. This demand spawned an important trade: the production of perfume and unguent vessels. Without these containers, perfume would have lost its fragrance and thus its value.

IV. POTTERY AND CONTAINERS

PERFUMES NEEDED SPECIALIZED vessels in which they could be easily transported and preserved. These vessels were used as funerary offerings and in everyday life. Some, as will be seen, were highly decorated and serve as works of art in modern museums.

Perfume and oil vessels are the most common perfume-related artifacts found at archaeological sites. Reasons for this are obvious as almost everyone had their own perfume and bottle. Indeed, tracing trade routes and the expanse of perfume is possible by plotting the occurrence of certain pottery pieces on a map of Mediterranean archaeological sites. This is especially true of Mycenaean perfumery and trade.[60] The style and shape of perfume vessels was in a slight way left to the imagination of the potter, but scientific principles were greatly responsible for dictating

[60] WILLIAM A. MCDONALD, *Progress Into the Past*, (New York: MacMillan Company, 1967), 325.

materials and shapes that would preserve the aromatic capabilities of perfume. Three phenomena were seen as detrimental to perfume: heat, sunlight, and evaporation.[61] Heat spoiled the perfume's fragrance by either undermining the oil base or making some other component rancid. The ability of sunlight to destroy certain organic substances was understood by the ancients, although they seem to have linked it with heat production. This is logical as they had no concept of radiation caused by the sun. Evaporation is an obvious harm as it would reduce the amount of liquid present and thus cause the aromatics to coagulate and settle, robbing the perfume of its odor. Theophrastus suggested vessels made of lead or alabaster because they were cool to the touch and did not leak. Clay and onyx were also used.[62]

The lekythos, aryballos, alabastron, askos, and pyxis were the common vessels for holding oil, cosmetics, perfumes, and unguents. Decoration for these vessels ran the gamut from toilet scenes to athletic contests. Describing these vessels textually would prove exhausting for the reader and author, thus the following pages, containing brief descriptions and illustrations, shall serve as the main explanation of these vessels.

---

[61] THEOPHRASTUS, 363.

[62] THOMPSON, 68.

LEKYTHOS (PL. LEKYTHOI)

Definition: A tall or squat vessel with a single handle and small, narrow neck.[63] These vessels are usually heavily decorated and are often found as grave goods. These vessels could range in height from 7 to 35 cm.[64] Lekythoi contained unguents, oils, and similar fluids.

Basic profiles: an early lekythos (far left); a shoulder lekythoi (left); a tall or neck lekythos (center); and a squat lekythos (right).

Types:[65]

Early:	Proto-Geometric to Archaic
One-piece:	Early 6th century B.C.
Tall or Neck:	Mid 6th century to 5th century B.C.
Squat:	Mid 5th century B.C. to end of Greek pottery

---

[63] BRIAN A. SPARKES, *Greek Pottery: An Introduction* (Manchester: Manchester University Press, 1991), 83.

[64] ROBERT S. FOLSOM, *Handbook of Greek Pottery* (Greenwich: New York Graphic Society, 1967), 175.

[65] FOLSOM, 175.

ARYBALLOS (PL. ARYBALLOI)

Definition: Spherical, spouted oil vessel. May or may not have feet.[66] Usually 5 to 13 cm in height.[67] Used to hold oils.

Basic aryballos profiles.

Types:[68]

| Corinthian: | 725 to 323 B.C. |
| Attic: | 700 to 323 B.C. |

---

[66] SPARKES, 80.

[67] FOLSOM, 177.

[68] FOLSOM, 177.

ALABASTRON (PL. ALABASTRA)

Definition: A small footless vessel with a narrow neck and a pouch- or sack-shaped holding cavity. Materials (perfumes and oils) were usually extracted with a slender stick.[69] Usually 7 to 20 cm long.[70]

Basic alabastra profile.

Types:[71]

No special types known, but there is a lot of variation based on period and geography.

---

[69] SPARKES, 80.

[70] FOLSOM, 178.

[71] FOLSOM, 178.

ASKOS (PL. ASKOI)

Definition: Arching handle and narrow spout.[72] Possibly used for oil. Usually 5 to 15 cm in diameter.[73]

General askos profile.

Types:

No special types known, but there is a lot of variety in shape.

---

[72] SPARKES, 80.

[73] FOLSOM, 179.

PYXIS (PL. PYXIDES)

Definition: Cosmetic box with a lid. Usually round, but with great variance in style and shape.[74] Usually 10 cm wide.[75]

Generalized Type III pyxis.

Types:[76]

Globular:	Proto Geometric
Pointed:	Early Geometric
Flat:	Late Geometric
Tall convex:	Proto Corinthian
Straight sided:	8th century Corinthian
Type I - Tripod:	6th century Attic

---

[74] SPARKES, 86.

[75] FOLSOM, 180.

[76] FOLSOM, 180.

Type II - Low concave sided:	Late 5th & 4th centuries Attic
Type III - High concave sided:	7th century Attic and Corinthian
Type IV - Normal or cylindrical:	4th century Attic and Corinthian

V. USES & PRACTICES

A S GREEK AND foreign perfumers perfected and differentiated their art, a wide variety of perfumes of various qualities was available. Although these substances had an obvious use, perfumes began to show up at a variety of events and were used in several capacities, not all of which used the perfume as an olfactory agent. Banquets and funerals used perfume. Doctors prescribed perfumes to cure everything from drunkenness to an obstructed bowel. By sheer volume, however, the use of perfume as a hygiene implement was its most common outlet.

The use of perfume and incense in funeral rites might have been the first use of aromatic substances by the Greeks. Exactly how perfume moved into secular use is not known with complete certainty. Greek funeral rites were complicated situations requiring access to large quantities of wood, aromatics, and food. Upon death, especially that of a warrior, a large stack of wood was created to serve as the fuel for the crematory fire. As the corpse burned, aromatics were thrown on the fire.[77] Although this had religious importance, it would not be out of bounds to assume aromatics were used to cover up the smell of a burning human. Libations of wine were poured. The bones and ashes of the funeral pyre were washed in wine. Once washed, they were mixed with scented oils or perfumes and placed in urns.[78] References to perfume use in funeral rites are present in several works of ancient literature. Homer's *Iliad* has one of the more famous instances. When Achilles rescues the Greeks who are trying to save Patroclus' body, a funeral of sorts is held. Achilles orders the following actions.

> He spoke, and bid the sad attendants round
> Cleanse the pale corse, and wash each honoured wound.
> A massy cauldron of stupendous frame
> They brought, and placed it o'er the rising flame ;
> They heap the lighted wood ; the flame divides
> Beneath the vase, and climbs around the sides.
> In its wide womb they pour the rushing stream;
> The boiling water bubbles to the brim.
> The body then they bathe with pious toil,
> Embalm the wounds, anoint the limbs with oil;[79]

---

[77] RIMMEL, 92.

[78] RIMMEL, 92.

[79] HOMER (trans. by ALEXANDER POPE), *The Iliad of Homer* (London: Cassell and Company, Ltd., 1909) pg. 341.

Stanley Lombardo, in his excellent translation of *Iliad*, approaches the concept of embalming the wounds differently than above and renders this last act thus:

And filled the wounds with a seasoned ointment.[80]

Perfume was of supreme importance to the dead. Hundreds of perfume vessels have been found as grave goods, with the graves of poorer persons having painted vessels when real ones were not possible. Graves account for a large quantity of the more decorated perfume vessels found.

Funeral rites are, by definition, religious. Aromatics had other uses in religious capacities. Sacrificial oxen, as seen in the *Iliad*, were covered in incense and burned. Further, aromatics were burned by priests and other officials in temples and at sacred locations. It might well have been a religious drive that brought perfume into the secular world. This drive may have been anything from emulation of a god or goddess to attempts at good luck or security. Perfume helped to comfort Hippolytus after Poseidon had exacted vengeance upon him.

---

[80] HOMER (trans. by STANLEY LOMBARDO), *Iliad* (Indianapolis: Hackett Publishing Company, Inc., 1997), pg. 366.

Ah, breath of divine fragrance! Even in the midst of evils I perceive thee, and my body is alleviated. Artemis the goddess is in this place.[81]

As is seen here and in other plays and literary works, the gods had a fragrant scent all their own. It signaled their presence and may, as in the case of Hippolytus, given comfort. It is possible that, to some, wearing perfume gave the same comfort. But to say that it always did would be to disregard a force more powerful than religion or fear: human vanity.

Feasts and banqueting, common forms of ancient Greek entertainment, used perfumes and unguents to make the dining situation more enjoyable. The wines served might be perfumed with rose or myrtle.[82] For the most part, this was done to make the wine more palatable as the Greeks, thanks to Theophrastus, who understood the connection between the senses of taste and smell. Another reason for perfuming wine was medicinal in nature: some perfumes were claimed to cure drunkenness, a common side effect of Greek culinary entertainment. Other strategies were used in dispensing perfumed substances at banquets. Pouches of aromatic flower petals, lily scented wash-basins, and scented lamp oil were used to set the

---

[81] EURIPIDES (trans. by MOSES HADAS and JOHN MCLEAN), *Ten Plays of Euripides* (New York: Bantam, 1960), 96.

[82] KENNETT, 71.

scene.[83] Xenophanes, a sixth century B.C. academic and philosopher, wrote of one ingenious host who covered doves with perfume and had them fly about the banquet hall, raining different perfumes down upon the guests.[84] Literary references to perfumes at banquets are quite common and account for most of the ancient references to aromatic substances. A typical dining scene has been preserved in a fragment of Xenophanes.

> For now the floor is clean as are the cups and hands of all.
> One puts on woven garlands;
> another passes along a fragrant ointment in a bowl.
> The mixing bowl stands full of cheer
> and another wine, flower fragrant in the jars, is at hand -
> which says it never will give out.
> In the midst frankincense gives forth its sacred scent,
> and there is cold water, sweet and pure.[85]

The exact reason why perfume was so pivotal to the Greek banquet scene is unknown. One possible theory

---

[83] KENNETT, 72.

[84] THOMPSON, 73.

[85] XENOPHANES OF COLOPHON (trans. by J.H. LESHER), *Fragments* (Toronto: University of Toronto Press, 1992), 11.

would again involve Theophrastus' idea that the senses of taste and smell are related. Perfume could have stimulated ancient appetites, much the same way the smell of charcoal makes most Americans salivate today. Another theory, just as plausible as the first, involves body odor. The Greeks did not bathe with any frequency, seeing the activity as a "remedial exercise."[86] As a result, bacteria trapped in the body's natural oils created body odor. This odor could be a problem. Banquet rooms were not necessarily very large. Confined spaces holding several people who might have done some unknown amount of physical exercise earlier in the day and who had no practical knowledge of disinfectant bathing could create an atmosphere that was almost caustic. Even to a people who were used to natural body aromas, the smell probably could have caused a loss of appetite. It is also possible, at some banquets, that the perfume was used in an attempt to gain a sexual partner. These theories are, at most, conjecture, but they do allow for more insight on the topic.

Perfume and unguents had an almost inherent medicinal benefit. Where perfume got its medicinal value is unknown, whether it be from some supernatural significance or from more worldly observations. Upon inspection, there is some validity to the idea that perfume, at least some of it, had

---

[86] KENNETT, 74.

medicinal properties, but perhaps for different reasons than given by the ancient Greeks. Theophrastus seemed to think that the medicinal qualities of perfumes lay in the spices used to make them.

> It is to be expected that perfumes should have medicinal properties in view of the virtues of spices; for these too have such virtues. the effects of plasters and of what some call 'poultices' prove what virtues they display, since they disperse tumours and abscesses and produce a distinct effect on various other parts of the body, on its surface, but also on the interior parts: for instance, if one lays a plaster on his abdomen and breast, the patient forthwith produces fragrant odours along with his eructations.[87]

Criton is credited with bringing perfume into the medical world. He was said to use fumigations of aromatic materials to cure illnesses. Hippocrates is also given credit for using a fumigation to end a plague of unknown character that ravaged Athens.[88] As medicine progressed, so did perfume's place in it. Certain perfumes were considered remedies for specific illnesses. Theophrastus denoted that megaleion was good for wounds and

---

[87] THEOPHRASTUS, 379 & 381.

[88] THOMPSON, 60.

swelling.[89] Oddly, this is plausible. Many perfumes were thinned with honey or wine. Honey, as recent research has shown, has a natural antiseptic capability. Wine, of course, has alcohol in it that reacts adversely with microscopic life forms. Thus, applying perfume to a wound had the same benefits as rubbing alcohol and peroxide do today. Further, as Theophrastus notes, many perfumes were astringent or caused tissue to pucker. This could, if it actually happened, stop bleeding and hinder introduction of infectious agents. Not all perfumes, with their perceived benefits, actually had a benefit. Theophrastus notes that rose perfume was good for the ears because it had salt, but he also states that it was good to cure a painful urinary condition called strangury.[90] This condition involves painful urination where the bladder is evacuated one drop at a time. It was thought that the salt in the rose-perfume would remove the supposed urethral blockage and allow normal urinary evacuation. When the blockage was gone, Theophrastus suggests that the fragrance would then cause the subject to urinate.[91] In actuality, the salt in the perfume would not have relieved any 'blockage'. In fact, if the strangury was bad enough and the subject was weak, the salt could lead to

---

[89] THEOPHRASTUS, 359.

[90] THEOPHRASTUS, 359.

[91] THEOPHRASTUS, 359.

fluid retention in body tissues and dehydration. Thus, it simply reduced the amount of fluid going through the body, but even slight relief from strangury was better than nothing. Iris perfume was said to be good for the body's other eliminatory function: defecation. Those who were constipated were to use iris perfume as it closed off the normal collection point of processed fluids, the bladder, and forced the liquids to collect in the colon and rectum.[92] The science behind this is false. Fluids do not 'back up' into the colon and rectum when the bladder ceases to function. Two interpretations of this cure are possible. The first would explain the concept that fluids collect in the colon and rectum. An obvious explanation would be diarrhea. The Greeks lacked knowledge of the germ theory of disease. Certain bacteria, viruses, and some foods cause diarrhea. The Greeks, who probably experienced this medical phenomenon, had to explain it. They realized that the body was evacuating wastes, so if a liquid was not coming out of the usual orifice, it had to be because that orifice was dysfunctional. As for the idea that increasing fluid content in the colon and rectum was a cure for constipation seems to show that the Greeks had knowledge of colonic irrigation. In extreme cases of constipation, it is necessary to imbibe large quantities of fluid into the colon and rectum to loosen a stool blockage. Ancient cultures the world

---

[92] THEOPHRASTUS, 359.

over used colonic irrigation as a remedy for illness, method of drug use, and for other purposes. Evidence of such a medical practice is Greece is questionable, but plausible.

Perfume was also singled out as causing illnesses also. Theophrastus found that megaleion, sweet marjoram, spikenard, and most of the cheap perfumes caused headaches.[93] Perfumes to this day cause some people to have headaches. Modern science has shown that certain people have allergic reactions to different materials, natural or synthetic. A usual manifestation of an allergic reaction is a headache, and in some cases what is called a migraine headache may also occur. It seems Theophrastus has documented a phenomenon that is all too familiar to anyone who is unfortunate enough to get a nose-full of cheap perfume or has had to run the aromatic gauntlet found in modern department store cosmetic areas.

Everyday use of perfumes and unguents in ancient Greece has not necessarily governed by fashion or any unwritten code of procedure. Rather, it was directed by personal preferences and ideology. There were as many different ways to apply perfume and unguents as there were people who applied them. Some ancient scholars and other learned people even attempted to formulate logical reasoning for their placement of perfume. Diogenes was one such scholar.

[93] THEOPHRASTUS, 365.

When you anoint your head with perfume it flies off into the air and only the birds obtain any benefit. But when applied to the legs and feet, the scent envelopes the whole body and gradually ascends to the nose.[94]

Logical practices for placing perfume on the body eventually, in may be argued, led to the formulation of elaborate bathing patterns. Antiphanes writes:

He bathes
In a large guilded tub, and steeps his feet
And legs in rich Egyptian unguent;
His jaws and breasts he rubs with thick palm oil
And both his arms with extract sweet, of mint;
His eyebrows and his hair with marjoram,
His knees and neck with essence of ground-thyme.[95]

Applying perfumes while bathing was not enough. Aromatic substances had to be applied periodically throughout the day if their scent was to be strong. It seems that locations for perfume application that are common today, like the wrist, where favored in ancient times as well. Theophrastus writes:

---

[94] GENDERS, 67.

[95] GENDERS, 69.

However there is one question which applies to all perfumes, namely, why it is that they appear to be sweetest when the scent comes from the wrist; so that perfumers apply the scent to this part. The explanation must be sought by observing what happens in the contrary case, inasmuch as heat changes or destroys the character of a scent, and the effect on the sense of smell is immediately perceived when perfumes are brought into close contact with the skin.[96]

This passage has been attributed to Apollonius by some authors, namely Thompson (1927). This is grossly incorrect as it comes from the works of Theophrastus. One point that the above argument does not consider is the mobility of the wrists. While walking, most people swing their arms. With the perfumed wrist being swung through the air, perfume molecules can evaporate from the skin and be inhaled, thus being smelled. This is not possible, however, without body heat. Theophrastus makes no mention of placing perfumes on the neck, but this may well have been practiced as it places the perfume in an area where an intimate would come across it during some type of social interaction. Theophrastus does note that perfumes with a strong odor are best placed on the head, with megaleion, Egyptian and sweet marjoram

---

[96] THEOPHRASTUS, 375.

being best.[97] It seems body chemistry is an important factor in how good a perfume smells. Theophrastus makes mention that some perfumes can "...become disagreeable and cause an even more unpleasant odor than the sweat, as though some sort of decomposition or decay took place."[98]

Many attempts were made to get a perfume's fragrance to hold to the body. Theophrastus suggested applying some perfumes while the body was relaxed for maximum benefit. Another method involved placing perfume in clothes and bedding. Theophrastus writes:

> When they make compound perfumes, they moisten the spices with fragrant wine; and this certainly seems to be useful for producing fragrance, seeing that perfumers also use it. These compound perfumes last a long time. They are used to impart a pleasant odor to clothes, while the powders are used for bedding, so that they may come in contact with the skin; for this kind of preparation gets a better hold and is more lasting so that men use it thus instead of scenting their bodies directly. Some, before putting the powder in the bedding, soak it in fragrant wine, so that it may acquire its scent: and some powders they moisten by mixing them

---

[97] THEOPHRASTUS, 375 & 377.

[98] THEOPHRASTUS, 377.

with mead and wine, or again simply with mead. For in general both these things help to give them fragrance.[99]

The methods of applying perfumes were too varied for anyone to make a complete list. The goal was to reduce body odor and to make oneself appear to be affluent and clean. Hygiene could be used to describe this process, but in reality the Greeks were no cleaner, they just masked the odors caused by body bacteria. The quest to smell better began to erode away the Greek ideals of virtuous physical work and exercise. Although perfumes and aromatics were used in funerals, religious rites, banquets, and as medical treatments, it was personal 'hygiene' that became the most important. This 'hygiene' turned its eyes to Greek society and began to clean out lower classes of people using the physical stimulus of smell to create a system of social stratification. Perfume and perfume use was to become one of the most contested issues in ancient Greece.

---

[99] THEOPHRASTUS, 379.

APPLYING PERFUMES AND UNGUENTS

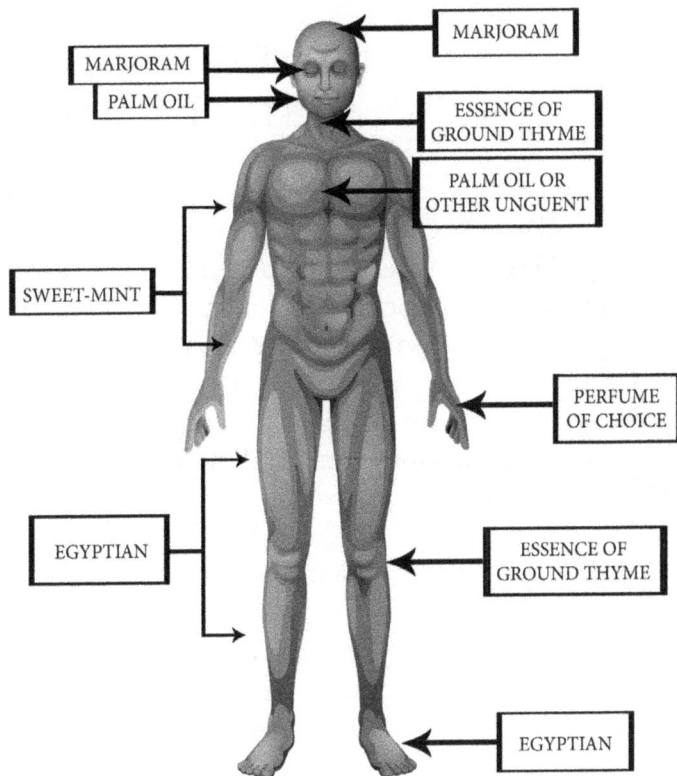

MARJORAM

MARJORAM
PALM OIL

ESSENCE OF
GROUND THYME

PALM OIL OR
OTHER UNGUENT

SWEET-MINT

PERFUME
OF CHOICE

EGYPTIAN

ESSENCE OF
GROUND THYME

EGYPTIAN

VI. SOCIETAL THOUGHT
& STRATIFICATION

PERFUME WAS ONE of the most popular products available in Greece. Perfume shops were social gathering places, frequented by different echelons of Greek society. Although it may seem a benign substance, perfume caused debate and division in Greek society.

Perfume was a debated topic at banquets and other gatherings of the educated. Legal attention was not given to the product until perfume was banned in 594 B.C.[100] Solon, during his legal reforms, made the sale and distillation of perfume illegal.[101] By outlawing the distillation of perfume, he theoretically prevented a perfumer from passing his trade on to his son, which was pursuant to another of Solon's laws. A hypothesis could be made that Solon hoped this would lead to

---

[100] KENNETT, 66.

[101] KATHLEEN FREEMAN, *The Work and Life of Solon* (Cardiff: University of Wales Press, 1926), 137.

the institutional extinction of the 'unguent-cookers'
he despised. His true reasoning is not exactly known.
Explanations for his actions suggest that he felt the
amount of money being spent by Athenians on foreign
luxuries such as perfume was too high.[102] Another
theory, a very plausible but unverifiable one, is that
Solon associated Greek perfume consumption with
the Persians. Since Persia proved to be Greece's enemy
in several conflicts, such emulation was seen as almost
treasonous.[103]

Solon's laws were impotent. There was no penalty
for continuing to produce perfume. If he had
instituted a penalty, the art might have been lost. With
no penalty and high profits to be made, perfumers
remained in business trying to satiate the Greek
demand for perfumes and aromatics. Perfumers held
an interesting position in Greek society. Despite their
contact with the rich and affluent, perfumers were
seen as one of the lowest classes.[104] A correlation to
modern times could be drawn with the relationship, in
the 1980s, of cocaine dealers and business executives.
Drug dealers were and still are a hated class by many
Americans, yet they had contact with some of the
richest and most powerful leaders of corporate and

[102] KENNETT, 66.

[103] MORRIS, 75.

[104] BRUN, 277.

political America. This relationship died off as drugs fell out of popularity in upper-class circles. What happened to perfume and its demand is lost to time. Perfumers' contact with the upper class was two-fold in purpose. First, perfumers supplied the rich with their favorite mark of distinction, expensive perfume. With this the rich could distinguish themselves from the poorer, malodorous classes. Second, an upper class patron was usually necessary to start of perfume business. Ingredients were often foreign and expensive. Financing a perfume shop was a prime investment opportunity for the already wealthy. Making a profit was almost guaranteed.

True criticism was leveled against perfume by the most educated Greeks: the philosophers. Socrates especially attacked perfume. Most of his criticisms of perfume were preserved by Xenophon and in Athenaeus' work, *The Deipnosophists*. Socrates was a critic of body hygiene in general. He disliked bathing and preferred the earthy man-musk of virtuous exercise. Socrates stated:

> For if a slave and a freeman be anointed with perfumes, they both smell alike; but the smell derived from free labours and manly exercise ought to be the characteristic of the freeman.[105]

---

[105] RIMMEL, 88.

This passage elucidates a real concern. It was the Greek ideal to exercise and conduct virtuous physical activities. The reward for this was admiration by one's peers and, according to Socrates, a certain odor. If everyone used perfume, the smell-badge of virtue was covered up. Soon, people might abandon, as they did, physical activity all together. Perfume made this possible. Since everyone used perfume, it was hard to tell who had exercised and who had not. Laziness, a direct violation of the Greek ideal, was the result. The concern that all might smell alike undermined the classist mentality of the ancient Greeks. In the early days of the perfume boom, aromatics were expensive. Only aristocrats could afford perfumes.[106] It was not until the 7th century that diversification in ingredients and sources allowed a wider spectrum of perfumes to be made. By the time of Theophrastus, 4th century B.C., there is a clear class of 'cheap' perfumes.[107] With the lower classes having access to perfume, aristocrats needed to seek further aromatic distinction for their position in society. Jean-Pierre Brun wrote that by the Hellenistic period, "What soon distinguished the aristocracy from the common people was not the use of perfumes but the quality and relative rarity of perfumes used."[108]

---

[106] BRUN, 277.

[107] THEOPHRASTUS, 365.

[108] BRUN, 277.

The result of this was the first system of social stratification based on a physical stimulus. Most systems of social stratification focused on birth or property rights as the determiner of class. In the perfumed world of the Greeks, these things held true, but were given impetus from perfume. The lower classes in Greece could raise their position if they were lucky. It was even possible for them to pretend they were of a higher stratum of society by dressing and acting differently. Perfume limited this by its expense. The rarest perfumes were expensive. Knock-off versions never smelled like the genuine article, thus the poor bound themselves to their social strata by perfume choice. This system of scent stratification has been present, intermittently, ever since. In the present day United States, class distinction is still exhibited by perfumes and aromatics. Varieties of perfumes sold at discount institutions are of poor quality. They do, as Theophrastus noted several centuries ago, cause headaches and many adverse effects, yet those who cannot access anything of higher quality use these low-grade substances with an almost religious zeal. A field study of this stratification in modern America would prove to be an educational, and possibly painful, endeavor. In Greece, it was much simpler.

It is important to keep in mind that perfume did not originate social division, but reinforced the preexisting system based on wealth and labor. Social and economic division in Greece was fairly simple compared to the attempts of other nations. The top of the social order was held by the landed wealthy who had slaves and laborers work their land.[109] Investments they made, sometimes even in perfume shops, multiplied their wealth. As trade developed, professional men (traders, craftsman, etc) rose in status at the time of Solon and were major players by the time of Pericles. The lower classes, usually small farmers, were troubled by poor farm land. Even though they may have owned their land, it was not productive enough to meet their needs.[110] These economic divisions controlled the purchasing power of the Greeks. What this power could buy when exercised reinforced the societal divisions. This division was not clearly organized or formulated, but was a byproduct of an economic phenomena that played on personal beliefs and perceptions about social class. Proving conclusively that this system was in fact known and participated in by the Greeks takes some dogged analysis.

Wealth, usually in the form of land, could be used as a financial base. With this base, the upper class could hold office and buy luxuries. Surplus income, regardless of time or culture, is usually absorbed by luxury purchases. Theophrastus tells us

---

[109] WILL DURANT, *The Life of Greece* (New York: MJF Books, 1939), 110.

[110] DURANT, 110-111.

of the existence of cheap perfume, and further tells that perfumes like megaleion had several expensive ingredients.[111] Theophrastus was a man of observation and logic, not given to social commentary, but his words betray his opinions about perfume segregation. He clearly denotes expensive and cheap perfumes. Granted, he does not fully explain the ramifications of each, but if he makes the distinction, others must have also. Simply put, the rich did not buy cheap perfume. Indeed, since sources like Brun (2000) put forth the concept that only the rich used perfume in the beginning and that cheaper varieties came later, thus causing distinct categories based on quality to be established. The production of cheaper perfume also coincides with the spread of perfume use. This spread can be seen in the quantity and type of grave goods left and with findings in urban excavations. As has been previously noted, there was even a class of people who could only draw perfume bottles on a tomb because they lacked the monetary resources to procure even the poorest aromatic. There is no stated system of perfume-based discrimination in the ancient sources. Socrates had his, but that is irrelevant to a point except that many of the banqueters in Athenaeus' work disagree with him and use the perfumes provided. Those writing about perfume, like Theophrastus and Apollonius, were interested in the science, not the

---

[111] THEOPHRASTUS, 355.

society. Others, like Athenaeus, were no real friends of those in a lower class. Thus commenting on another way to discriminate against them was futile. It was implied by the fact that different qualities of perfume existed. This is further reinforced by the fact that ingredients became important in perfume once cheaper varieties came into existence.[112] Why feel a need to shift importance if no system of perfume based stratification existed? The reason is that a system, evolving at times, did exist.

Ancient Greece may have led the way in physical stimulus discrimination. Other instances of it may exist in the historical record, but have yet to come to the light of modern scholarship. It must be admitted that perfume is but one of many determiners of social position and class assignment. Other factors could reassign position, for either good or ill. The fact that perfume was used as a marker for class makes it unique. It was an unspoken nametag. How rigid the system was is not known. Sources like Athenaeus and others are mysteriously silent. It is more than mere conjecture to assume that the system of distinction precipitated by perfume in ancient Greece was more serious than any modern distinction based on a physical stimulus. Class distinction in ancient Greece was what made their society function and, perhaps, malfunction.

---

[112]   BRUN, 277.

VII. FINAL THOUGHTS

THE FIELD OF HISTORY has changed during the past few decades. What were once considered fruitless areas of investigation are rapidly becoming the leading specialties in the field. Social phenomena like perfume have gone widely unnoticed in modern scholarship. Social history did not become a serious aspect of collegiate training and curricula until the 1990s. Studying a social character like perfume opens doors that might shed light on unknown facets of civilization.

Perfume, as a religious and social operant, created a system of worship, trade, mythology, and discrimination unique to a creator of physical stimulus. A complex social history and evolution is presented in perfume. From religious services and funerals to personal hygiene perfume developed into the 'must have' product of the ancient world. Due to its mystery and exotic ingredients, perfume was expensive. For a time only the wealthy could afford perfume, thus it became a mark of class distinction.

As materials and production diversified, cheaper perfumes were manufactured for the poorer peoples of ancient Greece. In their attempt to emulate the rich and step out of their social strata, poorer classes only cemented themselves in their caste. This holds true for modern populations as well.

Perfume sparked, according to some, a sense of laziness amongst the Greeks. Shirking on physical exercise became easy as no one smelled like virtuous physical activity. It has been suggested that this laziness and corruption of Greece ideals led to the fall of Greece society and a decay of their civilization. To say so absolutely would be a mistake, but it would also be an error to dismiss the effect of perfume altogether. It was an actor in a social drama that led to class discrimination and the death of a cultural tradition. When the reasons for the decay of Greek society are investigated, social operators like perfume must be considered in formulating an understanding of the decline. To not do so would be an error.

Perfume opened a new door to ancient Greece. In most historical work, events and people are well understood. But the common characteristics of daily life are often forgotten. Items like perfume and food are lost to time. Granted, we know what most civilizations consumed, but what did it taste like when they prepared it? What did it smell like? These questions open new doors that historians and archaeologists must enter together. Social history often lacks verifiable documentation. References do exist, usually in classical literature, to social phenomena. To understand these phenomena, historians, classicists, and archaeologists must work together to maximize the amount of information they can glean from the historical and archaeological record. Historians and archaeologists have a stewardship responsibility to make the most of their resources. It is academically and ethically sound.

What the true ramifications of perfume were in the ancient world are unknown. Some characteristics like social stratification can be theorized and surmised about, but other questions remain unanswered. Perfume came onto the scene fairly fast and seems to have left just as quickly. Although ancient authors wrote heavily on the subject, they are all mysteriously silent about the substance's decline. It may be that perfume did not decline. It did travel to the Romans who advanced the art in their own ways. There was a decline in the Middle Ages, at least in Europe. Middle Eastern peoples stilled used the substances as did European Jews. For this latter group, perfume played its old hand of social labeling that proved more deadly than it ever could have in ancient Greece.

The complete history of ancient Greek perfume is still being written. With archaeologists like Jean-Pierre Brun unearthing perfume shops and examining social characteristics of use and production, there may well be a renaissance in perfume studies. The authors of the first studies of perfume have passed on, but their scholastic endeavor remains. As archaeology and improved research methods open new avenues of research, the secrets of perfume might finally be revealed. True to form, perfume will not relinquish all its secrets because, after all, it is from the gods.

ALCHEMICAL TRADITIONS

FROM ANTIQUITY TO THE AVANT-GARDE

EDITED BY AARON CHEAK, PHD

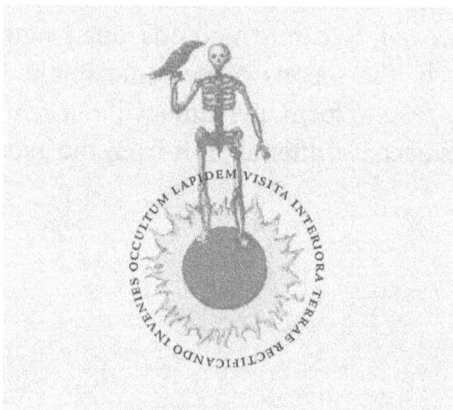

Sixteen Seminal Essays on the Alchemical Mysterium

Featuring both well-established scholars and emerging, cutting-edge researchers, this book synthesises a quintessentially high caliber of academic authorities on the vast and baroque heritage of the alchemical world. Drawn from international ranks and cutting across disciplinary boundaries, the contributors to this volume include some of the most gifted investigators into the world's esoteric lineages.

Featuring Aaron Cheak, Algis Uždavinys, Rodney Blackhirst, David Gordon White, Kim Lai, Sabrina Dalla Valle, Mirco Mannucci, Christopher A. Plaisance, Hereward Tilton, Angela Voss, Paul Scarpari, Leon Marvell, and Dan Mellamphy.

WWW.NUMENBOOKS.COM

KRATOS: THE HELLENIC TRADITION

ED. GWENDOLYN TAUNTON
NUMEN BOOKS 2013

Kratos contains the diversity and multifaceted components of thought which combine together to create the Hellenic Tradition – philosophy, mythology, archaeology, esotericism, mysticism, spirituality and paganism in the form of Hellenismos.

All of those topics are integral components in the rich and vibrant cultural heritage of Greece. Whilst some of these authors will delve deep into the ancient past via texts and archaeological discoveries, others will look towards the future for the Greek culture and keep their practices alive via Hellenismos.

Kratos therefore, contains articles for those who love the past and those who love the future and carry the Hellenic Tradition onwards as one on of the European continents oldest surviving Traditions.

WWW.NUMENBOOKS.COM

www.ingramcontent.com/pod-product-compliance
Lightning Source LLC
Chambersburg PA
CBHW030106180725
29799CB00022B/134